Fingers Finnigan

David Clayton

Illustrated by
David Mostyn

Contents

1 A goalkeeper problem

As Bert Fish drove to school he had a headache. He was the football coach at Penny Lane School. The school had a goalkeeper problem.

Fingers Finnigan was the team's goalkeeper. That was the problem!

Fingers was blond, tall and a brilliant goalie. But – and it was a very big but – he was also a joker. You never knew what he would do next. Sometimes, he would head the ball instead of catching it. Sometimes, he would bounce it on one fist.

Penny Lane were playing Green Park that morning. Green Park were the top team in the league and one point ahead of Penny Lane. It was the last game of the season. Penny Lane had to win to take the title.

How would Fingers play today? The only other goalkeeper, Wayne Groves, was off ill.

It was Fingers or no one.

Mr Fish got to school at 9.30 a.m. His team were waiting for him – that is, most of his team. Billy Chang, the big defender, was sitting on the steps. Harry Harrison, a fast wing-back, was leaning against the wall. Joe Sivori, the star striker, was booting a tennis ball against the door. The others were just hanging around. Fingers was not there. Mr Fish checked his watch.

One of the waiting players was Dean Pringle, the regular sub. If Fingers didn't show up, Dean would have to play. He was terrible in nets. Mr Fish couldn't bear to think about it.

Where was Fingers?

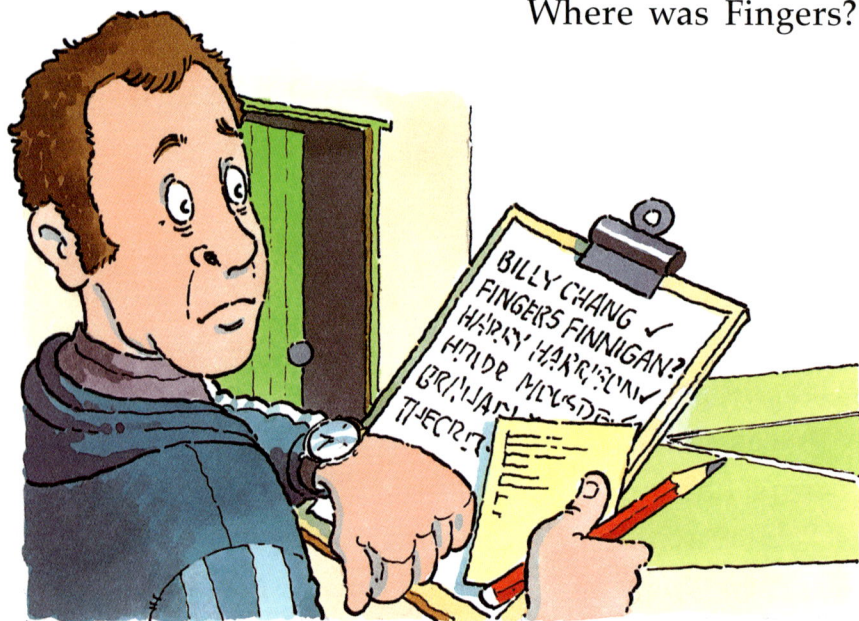

Mr Fish walked towards the team, but the team weren't looking at him. They were pointing past him and laughing.

Mr Fish turned around to see a Good Thing and a Bad Thing. The Good Thing was that Fingers was walking in through the gates. The Bad Thing was that he had a scruffy dog with him. Fingers was also wearing sunglasses. It was not sunny.

Mr Fish began to feel bad.

"What's this?" said Mr Fish pointing.

"It's a dog, sir . . ."

"I know that! But what is it doing here?"

"Ah, well, you see, sir. It's a long story . . ."

Mr Fish was sorry that he had asked.

". . . my gran has the flu." Fingers always had an answer to everything.

"So it's your grandma's dog?"

"No, sir, you see, she was minding the dog for her friend, Nora. Nora has a bad leg and can't . . ."

"Stop!" said Mr Fish. His headache was suddenly a lot worse. "I don't want to know all about your grandma's friends!"

"But what about Jess?" Fingers pointed to the dog.

"We can't be bothering with her now. We've got a match to play! Get her out of here!"

"But, sir, there's no time to take her home now! Gran said . . ."

Mr Fish had had enough of Fingers' story.

"That's enough about your gran!" he snapped. "And the dog."

Suddenly, there was a shout. A minibus was coming.

2 Green Park meet Fingers

"Look at that!" said Billy Chang. "Smart!"

Mr Fish turned to see a shiny, green minibus come to a halt. On its side it had "Green Park School" painted in large letters. Penny Lane's opponents had arrived.

The Penny Lane team went quiet, that is, except for Fingers.

"They're so big!" whispered Billy Chang. Fingers just laughed.

"Hey, don't forget I'm playing! No worries!"

Mr Fish shook his head. He was looking pale.

Fingers tied Jess to a bike stand. Then he strode into the school, grinning and joking.

Both teams headed for the changing rooms. A boy on the other team stared at Fingers' sunglasses.

"Why are you wearing sunglasses?" the boy asked.

"So I can see better when I take them off," explained Fingers, patting the boy on the head.

When Fingers put on his goalkeeper's kit, the Green Park lads goggled. Fingers had two enormous goalkeepers' gloves, one yellow and one red. He had a red baseball cap and a brilliant yellow and black jersey. He put on his lucky socks, one yellow, one red. Finally, there came his big, shiny boots.

"Who is that kid?" whispered one of the Green Park team.

"That's *Fingers Finnigan!*" hissed another.

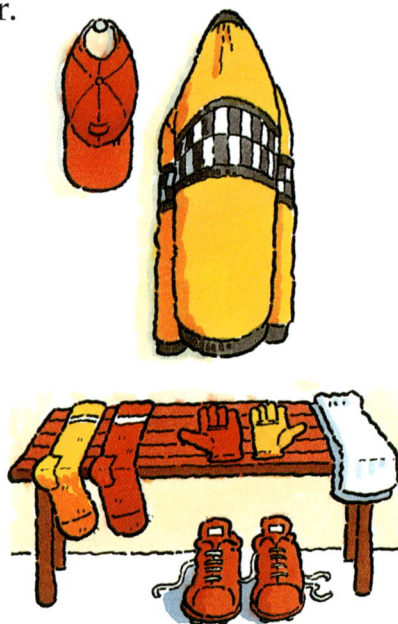

3 Fantastic Fingers

When the lads had changed, both teams ran across the road and on to the hilly park by the river. Pringle, the sub, ended up looking after Jess. It was time for the big match to begin.

Soon, the yellow shirts of Penny Lane were stuck in their own half. Green Park players seemed to be everywhere.

Suddenly, there was danger to Fingers' goal. Billy Chang gave away a free kick just outside the penalty area. Fingers organized a wall of players. Ricky Groves, a Green Park striker, took the kick.

Fingers dived to his left but the ball hit Billy Chang's head and went to Fingers' right. However, he flung his right leg up and clipped the ball against the bar with his right boot.

The ball went behind for a corner. Fingers caught the corner kick well, but there was nobody he could throw the ball to.

"Come *on!*" he yelled. "Do you want to win this game or not?"

He threw the ball to the half-way line. His team lost it yet again. Fingers was bouncing up and down on the goal line. He could hardly bear it. Then Penny Lane won a throw-in. Joe Sivori was just about to take it, when Fingers did something really mad.

"Mind the goal!" he shouted to Billy and ran off upfield!

"Are you crazy, Phillip?" yelled Mr Fish using Fingers' real name. "Get back!"

Joe Sivori was amazed to find his goalkeeper running towards him.

"Just give me that ball!" yelled Fingers.

Joe threw it down the wing to him and Fingers raced away. Green Park had never seen anything like it. Fingers was flying. Only Billy Chang was left in the Penny Lane half!

As Fingers charged on, a Green Park defender came up to challenge him. Fingers ran past him. Soon he was at the Green Park goal line. He raced for the goal.

Mick Miller, the Green Park keeper, came at him, and Fingers stopped. He groaned. Not one Penny Lane player was in the centre. Now five or six Green Park players were after him. Fingers had to kick the ball. He kicked it hard.

Del Cannon was racing back from the forward line to help the Greens' defence. But he was unlucky. The ball flew across, fast and low. Del couldn't get out of the way. The ball shot like a rocket off his boot and into his own goal. 1–0 to Penny Lane! Half-time, so far so good!
YEHHHHHH!!!!!!

4 Attack!
Attack!
Attack!

As soon as Penny Lane scored, it was a different game. Green Park weren't happy. They stayed back. Their two best players, Ricky Groves and Del Cannon, hardly touched the ball. Del looked very fed up after his own goal.

"Go on! Make it two!" yelled Fingers.

Now Penny Lane were on the attack. Fingers was itching to go up front again with the strikers, but Billy Chang kept pulling him back.

"Stop it, Fingers. You've got to stay in goal. We *have* to win!"

Fingers walked up and down the goal line. He swung on the bar. He wandered around the goal area. He sang to himself. Everyone else was charging upfield. He didn't have a thing to do.

Play at the other end of the pitch got better and better. Joe Sivori scored a penalty making it 2–0! Fingers was dying for more action. It was a dangerous time for his team – Fingers was bored.

Soon, Penny Lane won a corner. Fingers raced upfield and this time Billy could not stop him. As the corner came over, Fingers ran in to head the ball. It flew towards the top corner of the goal. A defender headed the ball over the bar. Corner again!

"Get back, Phillip!" shouted Mr Fish.

Fingers took no notice. He stayed in the Green Park penalty area. Over came the ball again. There was a scramble in front of the goal. The ball skidded around like a bar of soap. Then it flew out for yet another corner to Penny Lane. Green Park held on. Now even Billy Chang came up into the attack. The Penny Lane half was empty.

Then Joe Sivori headed the ball straight at the goal mouth. It just clipped the bar and bounced back into Mick Miller's arms. He booted the ball hard downfield.

The goalkeeper's kick flew out to Green Park's right wing. Del Cannon was racing after it. This could be dangerous.

Billy Chang could not get across. Fingers raced towards his own area. He was scared. Way ahead of him, the goal was wide open. He had given Green Park a great chance. Del Cannon was clean away.

"Stop him!" Fingers yelled as he sprinted on.

Del Cannon slowed and looked up at the goal thirty metres away. He took aim, booting the ball as hard as he could.

Fingers was back in his own area. *I mustn't make a mess of things*, he thought. *I've got to save it!*

But the ball was flying towards the goal. Fingers dived desperately, but it skimmed his hand and went into the net. Disaster!

5 Worse and worse

As Fingers picked the ball out of the net, Green Park were cheering and Penny Lane were shouting. They were shouting at Fingers.

"What did you do that for, you fool?" yelled Billy Chang.

"We scored the last time I did it," replied Fingers, kicking the ball back to the centre.

"We were winning easily," said Billy. "Now, if they score one more goal, we've lost the league."

Fingers walked back feeling very small. He huddled his body with his arms. He knew that he had made a terrible mistake, but he also knew that his first rush upfield had led to a goal. He couldn't help it. He always rushed at things. He was like that.

Fingers' heart sank. He could see that his team were scared. Now they got rid of the ball as if it was a time bomb. However, Penny Lane were still winning 2–1. In five minutes they would be champions. Then everyone would forget Fingers' bad mistake.

Suddenly, a Green Park defender swung the ball high downfield. Ricky Groves raced down the middle after it.

"Come out, Phillip!" screamed Mr Fish.

"COME OUT, FINGERS!" Now the whole world seemed to be shouting at him again.

The ball was bouncing high. Fingers ran right at it. BAM! There was a purple blur. He went in with his fists and Ricky Groves was down.

"Penalty!" shouted the referee, pointing to the spot.

6　Disaster

Fingers was in tears. "Oh no!" he cried.

"I should send you off," said the referee.

"But, sir," said Ricky Groves, who had now got up and was rubbing his face. "We both went for it. I just got there first."

"Thanks," said Fingers.

"Don't thank me, yet!" said Ricky, putting the ball on the penalty spot.

People began shouting. "Come on Fingers, you can save it!"

"Come on Fingers, one more save!"

Mr Fish hid his face.

Ricky stroked his curly, brown hair and stood very still. Fingers bounced like a huge, blond spider. The whistle went. Ricky took three slow paces then struck the ball with his foot. Fingers leaped to his left.

Fingers got a hand to the ball but it flew up under the bar and in. Goal! 2–2.

Fingers had made two brilliant saves and at least five good ones. He had almost saved the penalty. He had scored a goal. But he had given away two goals.

The game went on, but Penny Lane's attack got nowhere. Four minutes later, the whistle went. Green Park were champions. Fingers had given the game away.

The champions yelled. Penny Lane gave them three cheers then walked off the pitch sadly. All except Fingers. He stayed in his goal and stared at the empty pitch. He'd done his best, but it had all turned out wrong.

Fingers felt something suddenly touch his leg. Something was licking him. Jess! Dean Pringle must have let her go. Fingers picked up the little dog. She licked his face until he could hardly see. He felt like crying.

He walked very, very slowly back to school. He crept into the changing room. The others did not even turn to look at him. Green Park were singing, shouting and laughing. He could not bear to watch.

As Fingers got changed, he felt a pat on the back. He turned to see Ricky Groves standing there. The boy had a lovely black eye where Fingers had hit him.

"Bad luck, Fingers. You're still a great goalie!"

"Well done, Ricky!" Fingers replied.

Fingers was glad that someone had spoken to him. He felt very lonely.

Mr Fish stood near the door with his head in his hands.

"Sorry, sir!" said Fingers as he passed.

"OK, Phillip," Mr Fish said sadly.

Soon, Fingers was out in the cold street with Jess. They were on their way back to Gran's. She would want to see if he had looked after Nora's little dog properly.

Usually, the team went for hot-dogs together. Today, they had all gone straight home. Fingers was glad to have Jess with him. He felt foolish, sad and cold. Throwing the game away like that really hurt.

7 No more football!

Fingers liked going to his gran's. His mum worked at the card shop on Saturdays and his dad played for a local football team. Sometimes, Fingers watched him, but he couldn't bear any more football today.

Gran's face lit up when she saw Fingers and Jess. She was sitting in an armchair, wrapped in a blanket. Fingers gave her a hug.

Grandad was watching horse-racing on TV.

"Well then," he said. "How did you get on?"

"We drew 2–2 against the top team."

"Oh, not bad, eh!" The old man's eyes went back to the TV screen. Fingers did not explain that Penny Lane had to win to be champs.

"Would you like a piece of cake, Phillip?" asked Gran.

"Yes please, Gran, I'm starving!" Fingers sat down beside her.

The horse race started. Grandad shouted all the way through.

"Come on, Golden Lad! Come on!" Then he groaned.

"Terrible!" he said. "Terrible! They should have that horse on the beach at Blackpool. What a donkey!"

Fingers laughed. Grandad was hopeless at picking horses. Suddenly, Grandad smiled.

"Here you are. Just for you!" He pressed the remote control to put the football on TV.

"Thanks, Grandad," said Fingers. What else could he say?

Every kick, every goal, reminded him of the championship he had just thrown away. First, they showed great goals, which wasn't too bad. But then they showed terrible mistakes by goalkeepers . . .

"Did you see that? What a fool!" laughed Grandad. "I bet you never make stupid mistakes like that!"

The words stung Fingers. He remembered what Billy Chang had shouted at him. "You fool!"

Fingers was miserable. He didn't want to think about the game. He ate his cake and drank his tea. He watched football for a bit to please Grandad. Finally, he stood up and took the dog's lead.

"I think I'll take Jess to see Nora."

"That's very kind of you," said Gran.

I've got to be on my own for a while, Fingers thought. *I'll just keep walking until I feel a bit better about everything.*

8 Fire!

It was a gloomy afternoon. Fingers pulled his hat over his eyes and tucked his hands in his pockets. He walked in a daze up Highgate Hill, over to Broken Cross, and then through Stanley Park. The world was grey, everything was so grey. He put his headphones on, pushed the sound of his personal stereo up high, and stomped on.

Eventually, he came to Sandy Lane, where Nora lived. In the distance he could see a glow in the gloomy afternoon. Fire? At Nora's? He pulled off his headphones. People were shouting. In a second, Fingers was racing towards the light, with Jess running after him. After a hundred metres, he saw that it was beyond Nora's house. Jess started to bark madly.

It *was* a fire. A crowd had gathered. They were all pointing, staring. But nobody was *doing anything!*

Fingers saw Nora in the crowd at once, and handed Jess over to her.

"Who lives there, Nora?" asked Fingers, pointing to the house.

"Young Karen with her baby. We think she's still inside."

"We've got to get her out!" he yelled.

Suddenly, the front window shattered, flames belched out and everyone stepped well back. As Fingers approached, the heat of the flames made his eyes water.

"It's hopeless!" said a little man with a moustache. "We'll never get her out of there!"

"We don't even know for sure that Karen's in the house," said a woman.

"There she is!" There was a shout.

"Help! Please help us!" a girl screamed from an upstairs window, waving her arms frantically.

The crowd froze with horror. Not one person took a step towards the house.

"Do something!" shouted Fingers. "DO SOMETHING!"

"We've rung the fire brigade," said a tall man.

"Is that all? Get a ladder. Come on!" urged Fingers.

"We have rung," repeated the man.

"Useless!" snarled Fingers.

"Don't talk to me like that! We've done all we can!" said the man.

More smoke and fire poured out of the downstairs windows. They could hardly see the girl now.

Fingers turned away from the crowd. To the right of the girl's window, there was a grey, plastic drainpipe. He sprinted in and tried to shin up it. It was slippery and creaky. He could feel his face crackling in the heat like burnt bacon. The left arm of his jacket was sizzling and smoking. After getting about two metres up, the drainpipe broke with a crack and he came crashing down. As he hit the floor, flames roared out over his head.

Fingers rolled away and realized that his hair was on fire. He rubbed his head on the wet grass. Nora helped him beat out the flames with her coat. Then he leaped up. He'd been foolish and that wouldn't help anyone. Now, he'd got to think – and think fast.

"A ladder," he shouted. "Get a ladder!"

His voice was croaky from the smoke. One or two men came a bit closer, yet *still* they stood there with pale faces, doing nothing.

Now Fingers felt desperate. He felt no pain from his burns, only a rage that no one was doing anything.

He ran round to the back of the house. No ladder! He ran down the back alley looking for one, jumping over fences into people's yards.

"Hey, lad, what do you think you're doing?" yelled a man, coming out of his back door.

"Please help me! I'm trying to find a ladder," gasped Fingers. "There's a girl and baby trapped in that house there!"

"I haven't got a ladder," said the man, but he ran with Fingers back to the house.

By the time they got there, the girl and her baby were completely hidden in the smoke.

Fingers was frantic. He had to do something, but what?

Fingers felt the front door. It was cool. They could try to break it down. Fingers and the man hurled themselves against the door. The man hurt his shoulder.

They grabbed a garden gate and tried to break the door down again. It was no good.

Flames lit up the hall behind the door. It was too late to open it now.

"Help!" a shrill scream came again from the upstairs window. "We can't get out!"

Fingers could not even hear a siren yet. The fire brigade was nowhere near.

Suddenly, flames came bursting out of the front door. Everyone screamed and backed away. Fingers was running out of ideas.

"Jump, just JUMP!" he yelled to the girl.

"Not . . . with . . . my baby!" she cried.

Fingers ran up close to the house.

"Throw the baby down," he yelled, "then jump yourself."

"Will you catch her?" cried the girl.

"Yes, yes!" he yelled. "I'm a goalie!"

Another BOOM came from deep inside the house. More flames burst from the windows. The girl screamed.

In the heat, Fingers could feel his skin go tight. He could feel his eyeballs go tight. Still the girl did not throw her baby down. Fingers' clothes were smoking. His head was boiling hot. His mind was swirling. He felt himself going faint.

"NOW!" he yelled. "THROW HER! NOW! GO ON!"

The baby sailed through the smoky air. Fingers stood firm. He never took his eyes off the orange bundle as it flew towards him.

Fingers got the catch just right. He did not snatch at the baby. Instead, he hugged her to his chest as she thudded into him.

As he fell backwards, the baby was safe in his arms. He twisted her away from the sizzling heat of the flames.

"YES!" he gasped. "YES!"

Suddenly he realized that he was not alone. Two figures were dragging them both clear. Firefighters! The next few moments were like a dream. A fire officer was staring down at him. Fingers' mouth had bubbled up with blisters. He could only croak, "Baby? Girl?"

"Yes," said the officer, "they're both OK."

In the ambulance, the pain started to bite. Fingers rolled over and saw that the young woman was there, too. He wanted to speak, but he couldn't. She dragged herself over to him, coughing badly.

"Thank . . . you!" she croaked.

Though his face was black and as hard as plastic, Fingers smiled at her.

He had scored a goal and lost two, been a fool and lost a championship, but he had made a catch and saved a life. What was a football game compared to that?

Fingers was in hospital for a very long time, but after a few days he had a visit from the Penny Lane team. Nora was there, too, telling everyone what had happened.

". . . and he caught the baby as he stood there with his clothes smoking!"

"Tell you what, kid," said an older boy in the next bed, "you should be a goalkeeper if you can catch like that!"

They all just laughed.